The FBI
Democracy's
Guardian

BY JAMES McCAGUE

GARRARD PUBLISHING COMPANY
CHAMPAIGN, ILLINOIS

Library of Congress Cataloging in Publication Data

McCague, James.
    The F.B.I.: democracy's guardian.

    1. United States. Federal Bureau of Investigation—
Juvenile literature. I. Title.
HV8141.3   364.12'06173   73–9790
ISBN 0–8116–6508–9

Picture credits:

Brown Brothers: pp. 4, 12, 20 (both), 27 (top), 30,
    36 (both)
Culver Pictures: p. 17
Federal Bureau of Investigation: pp. 1, 9, 45, 57,
    67 (both), 70, 81, 84 (all), 85, 89 (both), 92
United Press International: pp. 27 (bottom), 48,
    53, 60, 76

Contents

President Roosevelt's concern with the nation's natural resources took him far from Washington. He set up the Bureau of Investigation in order to protect these resources from lawbreakers.

1. The President's Big Stick

President Theodore Roosevelt was angry. Right in the middle of one of his hardest fights, the Congress of the United States had turned against him.

Seven years earlier, in 1901, Roosevelt had entered the White House determined to stop the thieves and dishonest politicians who were robbing the American people of millions of dollars in natural resources. Some of the worst abuses concerned public lands. Millions of acres in California, Oregon, and other western states had been set aside as national forests belonging to all Americans. But many of the huge corporations of those days cared nothing about the people's rights. These businesses were wealthy and powerful. They found it easy to bribe dishonest government officials, who helped them steal valuable timber and mining lands through all sorts of frauds. So widespread was the practice that it had become a national scandal.

President Roosevelt was a strong, courageous president, a man of action rather than words. "Speak softly and carry a big stick" was his motto. He had ordered the U.S. Department of Justice to make a thorough investigation of the land frauds.

It started off very well. The Department of Justice had no detectives of its own at that time, but Secret Service agents "borrowed" from the Treasury Department soon uncovered plenty of evidence. Dozens of the guilty men were caught and sentenced to prison. Some had held high government positions, and this fact made the affair all the more shocking. Several of the investigators loaned by the Treasury Department turned out not to be Secret Service men at all, however, but only private detectives hired for the job. Some were not even good detectives. A few were suspected of having criminal records themselves. Such things made the whole investigation look bad. There was little doubt that many innocent people had been made to suffer along with the guilty ones.

The full story came out years later.

But even at the time, some congressmen began to grow suspicious. Rumors sprang up that President Roosevelt was organizing a secret police force, something no democratic government could tolerate. There never was a scrap of proof for such rumors. In May of 1908, nonetheless, Congress drew up a law forbidding the Department of Justice, and all other government departments, to use Secret Service agents.

Roosevelt protested bitterly. His attorney general, Charles J. Bonaparte, pointed out that the Department of Justice would be of little use to the nation without some means of collecting evidence against lawbreakers. Congressmen refused to listen. They passed the law, in the form of an amendment to a bill too important for the president to veto.

The office of the attorney general in 1908—and
the first home of the Bureau of Investigation

Theodore Roosevelt, the man with the
big stick, was not easily beaten, however.
He called Bonaparte to the White House
and told him to create a force of agents
responsible to the attorney general alone,
"subject to no other department or bureau." On July 26, 1908, Attorney General Bonaparte issued the necessary order.
Thus, quietly, without much publicity or

fanfare, the organization to be known as the Bureau of Investigation began.

Under a new president, William Howard Taft, Congress's worries over a secret police force faded away. In 1910 the first of a series of new laws was passed, giving the bureau power to investigate certain crimes against the federal government. Its powers were strictly limited, but the bureau's duties were quite limited too. Thus it remained small and almost unknown to the average American citizen.

An era was drawing to a close, however, during these early years of the twentieth century. A war was brewing across the sea in Europe. When it came, it would be greater and more terrible than anyone could foresee. Among other things, it would bring a time of testing to the Bureau of Investigation.

2. The Learning Years

It was past midnight on a July morning in 1916. Black Tom Island lay dark and still in New York Harbor. Then suddenly a great explosion broke the silence. A fiery glare lit up the sky. Another explosion followed, and another and another, each louder than any thunderbolt. A hundred miles away, sleeping people awoke and tumbled from their beds. In New York City and across the harbor in New Jersey, tall buildings rocked and swayed and windows burst into splinters.

The Bureau of Investigation had its first problem of World War I.

Luckily, only four people died on Black Tom. But thousands of tons of shells, bombs, and other explosives, ready to be loaded aboard ships bound for Europe, had been stored on the island. Nothing was left but blackened, smoking ruins.

World War I had been going on in

A fireboat wets down the still smoking wreckage of Black Tom Island.

Europe since 1914. On one side was a powerful group of nations led by Germany. Opposed to them was a group known as the Allies: mainly England, France, and Russia. The United States stayed out of the war at first, though most Americans favored the Allies. America had become an important source of war materials for England and France. The Black Tom explosions were set off by German secret agents with orders to prevent such help. Since the early months of the war, in fact, German agents had been active in the United States.

When this country finally declared war on Germany in 1917, these German agents were well prepared and ready to stop at nothing. Catching them became the duty of the Bureau of Investigation.

It was a difficult job, for the United States was not ready for war. The bureau had only about 300 agents at this time. Though most of them were brave and honest, they were not well organized, and they had neither the training nor the experience to fit them for tracking down enemy agents. Nor could they count on any help from outside. The Secret Service already had more work than it could handle. The U.S. Army's intelligence service consisted of just four men. The navy had only a few officers assigned to intelligence work.

On the other hand, there were many German spies, carefully trained and skillful at sabotage. The disaster on Black Tom Island was soon followed by other acts of destruction. Important bridges and railroad tracks were blown up.

Bombs were planted in the holds of cargo ships, and timed to go off far out at sea. Factory machinery was damaged, to stop or slow down war production.

The Bureau of Investigation did its very best. A hundred new agents were added to the force. Even then there were not enough for all that needed to be done. The bureau tried to keep track of people who had come to this country from Germany and Austria-Hungary. Most of these people had become American citizens, but some had not yet done so. They were called "enemy aliens." Because a few of the aliens wanted Germany to win the war, it was necessary to watch them all. In addition, special agents had to protect harbors, docks, and factories doing war work. They had to trace thousands of men who deserted from the army and navy, and other thousands who ran away to keep from being drafted into the service. All these things, added to the bureau's normal peacetime duties, made a heavy load to carry.

Yet if this was a time of harsh testing, it was a time of learning too. Experience was a good teacher. The bureau made many mistakes, but it also had some great successes. In New York City, agents led by a supervisor named Charles DeWoody discovered secret German code books which helped them to break up a spy ring there. In other cities, German agents were caught or forced to leave the country. Considering the overall record, all the same, it was lucky for the bureau that Germany was defeated on the battlefields of Europe. She surrendered in November 1918.

Armistice Day, 1918, marked the end of World War I and the beginning of a new series of problems for the Bureau of Investigation.

Peace brought great changes to America. The war left many people in a restless, discontented mood. Slowly they began to realize that the old times before the war were gone forever. As war work stopped, hard times came to the United States. Factories shut down. Workers lost their jobs, or had their pay cut. Strikes and riots broke out in many cities. Before long it appeared that much of the disorder was caused by organized groups with selfish goals of their own. Some believed that workers alone ought to run the country. Others were anarchists, opposed to government of any kind. Still others, about whom little was known as yet, were Communists.

Toward the war's end, Russia had suffered a violent revolution. After months of bloodshed and confusion, a party led by Nikolai Lenin took control of the Russian government. Its members called themselves Communists, and said that they were for rule by all the people. But leaders in most other countries were not sure of these Communists.

In the United States a special division of the Department of Justice was ordered to make a study of the people behind the violent troubles that were taking place. A young attorney who had joined the department in 1917, fresh from law school, was put in charge. His name was John Edgar Hoover.

As he followed through on the project, Hoover became sure that Communism was much more than just a political belief. Instead, he felt that it was a far-reaching conspiracy, or plot, directed by the new rulers of Russia. Their aim was

This explosion on Wall Street in September 1920 was one of several in the postwar years. Incidents like these led to raids on aliens suspected of being Communists. These were led by Attorney General A. Mitchell Palmer (left).

nothing less than the overthrow of other nations' governments, by force if necessary. The young attorney wrote this in his report.

It was the first blow in Hoover's lifelong battle against the enemies of his country.

Attorney General A. Mitchell Palmer acted on the report at once. He ordered a series of raids to round up all aliens thought to be either Communists or anarchists. Special agents of the Bureau of Investigation carried out the raids, and nearly 700 men and women were sent back to Russia in the three years from 1919 to 1921. But the raids were badly handled. Far too many people were falsely accused, taken unlawfully from homes, and denied their rights to honest trials. When this came out it caused a storm of protest from fair-minded citizens everywhere.

The Red Scare, as it was called, finally ended in ill will and misunderstanding. Attorney General Palmer took full blame for all the mistakes that had been made. Still, the Bureau of Investigation had not looked very good in its first brush with Communism.

There would be others, though.

3. The Turning Point

By election time in 1920 Americans had grown weary of labor troubles and violence. When Senator Warren G. Harding of Ohio ran for president on a promise to take the country "back to normalcy," the voters elected him by a large majority.

Promising, though, was a long way from doing.

Harding was likable and well-meaning, but he did not have the qualities that would have made him a strong president.

Instead of seeking the best men he could find to serve in his cabinet, he chose old friends. They, in turn, appointed friends of their own to the departments under their control. Since few of these men were really fitted for the jobs they held, there soon was confusion throughout the government. It was not long until men who were actually dishonest wormed their way into government jobs too. Soon stealing and cheating became common.

The Bureau of Investigation was one of the first to suffer in the new setup. William J. Burns took over as its director in August 1921. At first, he looked like a good choice. For many years Burns had run the famous private detective agency that was named after him. He seemed to know his business. Yet Burns's record was far from spotless. Working people did not trust him, because he had often taken part in labor disputes on the side of their bosses. His detectives had beaten up striking workers and wrecked their union offices. Burns himself had been accused of trying to bribe jury members in one very important court case. Most people had heard very little about all that, though, and Burns had many friends in the government.

Soon after taking charge, he began to bring his friends into the bureau as special agents. Very few of them made good agents. Some were men with shady backgrounds. But old hands in the bureau could only mind their own business, steer clear of the new men, and carry on. One who did so was young J. Edgar Hoover, now assistant director of the bureau.

Conditions around the country, in the meantime, failed to get better. President Harding's campaign slogan, "back to normalcy," began to sound like a sad joke. Everywhere, people worried over the spreading rumors of dishonesty in Washington. Congressional investigations started. Little by little, the evidence piled up, and the whole ugly tale came out. By one means or another, dishonest officials in several different departments had robbed the government—robbed all the nation's people, in other words—of millions of dollars. It was a worse situation than the one Theodore Roosevelt had had to deal with twenty years earlier.

President Harding never knew how badly the friends he trusted had deceived him. He fell ill and died quite suddenly in August 1923. It was Vice President

This cartoon of the twenties showed the Senate "airing" the scandals arising in government during the presidency of Warren G. Harding, seen below.

Calvin Coolidge, stepping into the country's highest office, who had to clean up a national scandal.

Nearly a year later J. Edgar Hoover was called to the office of his boss, Harlan Fiske Stone. Stone had been appointed attorney general by Coolidge only a few weeks before. He was a tall, ruggedly built New Hampshire man and one of the most respected lawyers in the United States. Years later, Hoover often told close friends that he half-expected to be fired that day. He knew that William J. Burns was already gone, and that Stone was out to clean up the Bureau of Investigation. Hoover's own record was good. Still, it was always possible that he might be blamed for some of the things Burns had done.

The attorney general wasted no time

in getting to the point. He had picked Hoover, he said, as acting director of the bureau. Would he take the job?

"Yes, sir," the young man said, after a moment's thought. "But only if certain things are understood."

Gruffly Stone ordered, "Name them."

First, said Hoover, he would take his orders directly from the attorney general himself, and from no one else. The bureau must never be forced to give in to the wishes of important politicians, or be made to work for politicians. Such things had happened much too often in the past. Finally, all special agents would be hired and promoted on merit alone.

Stone nodded curtly. "I wouldn't have it any other way," he said.

The date was May 10, 1924, a turning point for the Bureau of Investigation.

J. Edgar Hoover, newly appointed director of the
Bureau of Investigation, was determined to make
the bureau a strong and effective organization.

4. Hoover Takes Charge

J. Edgar Hoover knew the difficulties he faced. He was only 29, a young man still—perhaps *too* young to head an important government bureau. For that reason alone, many people believed the attorney general had made a mistake in choosing him. Hoover knew that. He knew also that some congressmen were disgusted by the conditions that had existed under William J. Burns. They wanted to do away with the Bureau of Investigation altogether. If Hoover failed to make good, there might be no second chance—for him or anyone else.

He went to work, resolved not to let that happen.

Getting rid of dishonest and inefficient agents was the first thing to be done. The new director already knew those who had been hired by Burns. He fired them at once. But for years before Burns's time the practice of employing agents because they had friends in the government had been common. Many such agents had never really done their jobs, and never would. So Hoover set himself the long, tiresome task of studying the record of every man in the bureau. The good ones would be kept on, even promoted. The bad ones would have to go. And go they did.

At first this caused trouble. Agents

who lost their jobs often wrote to their congressmen, or to other important people who had helped them get their jobs in the first place. Angry protests poured into the bureau. Powerful politicians threatened to see that Hoover himself was kicked out. But he refused to back down, and Harlan Fiske Stone stood behind him in every case. Slowly it became clear that both men meant business: there would be no politics in the Bureau of Investigation.

Hiring rules were tightened up. New men looking for jobs were thoroughly checked to make sure that they were honest and reliable. Hoover had some additional ideas about hiring, also. The collecting of evidence was certainly a necessary part of every special agent's duties. Yet the records showed that some lawbreakers went free only because agents did not know how to build strong cases against them. Under Hoover's new rules, therefore, all agents had to be trained in either law or accounting.

In past years, special agents who worked in field offices all over the country had reported directly to Washington, D.C. Their local supervisors often knew very little about what they were doing. J. Edgar Hoover quickly put a stop to that. Special agents in charge of the field offices were made responsible for the men under them and given the power they had lacked before. Rules of conduct were laid down, and enforced.

Slowly a strong, smooth-running organization took shape. An Identification Division was created in 1924. It was built around a fingerprint file turned over to the bureau by federal prison authorities at Leavenworth, Kansas. Later, several local police departments added their fingerprint cards to the file. For the first time, known criminals anywhere in the United States could be identified quickly and easily. Later still, a laboratory was opened in bureau headquarters, to develop the newest and best methods of scientific crime-fighting. Both the laboratory and the Identification Division were placed at the service of any state or local police force that needed help.

Attorney General Stone kept a sharp eye on his young director, and he liked what he saw. Within a year Hoover's appointment was made permanent. Shortly afterward President Coolidge selected Stone himself as a justice of the United States Supreme Court. Still Hoover and his

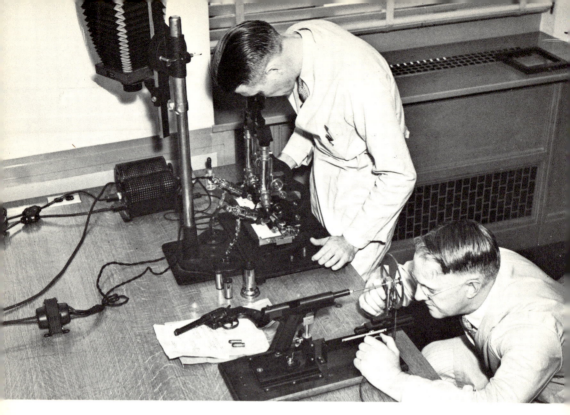

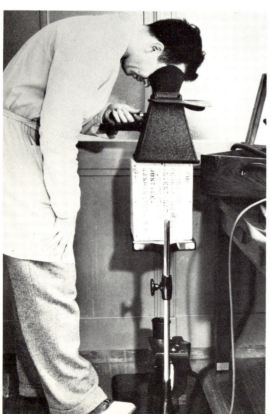

The bureau at work in the early 1930s: X-raying a package to make sure it does not contain a bomb (left) and identifying bullets by means of a microscope.

former boss remained close friends. As Stone said in a letter written in 1932:

> It is always a comfort to me to see how completely you have confirmed my judgement. . . . The Government can now take pride in the Bureau.

That was quite true. J. Edgar Hoover had built the Bureau of Investigation into an effective, impartial weapon of law enforcement. With only 326 agents, it was not very large. But they were all good men, who took pride in themselves and in the organization of which they were a part.

It was none too soon. By the early 1930s the United States was caught deep in a new era of crime.

5. The Time of the Gangsters

On a June day in 1933 four passengers
stepped from a railroad train in Kansas
City, Missouri. Two of the men were special agents of the Bureau of Investigation. Another was the police chief of a
town in Oklahoma. The fourth man wore
handcuffs. He was Frank Nash, a convicted bank robber and murderer who
had escaped from federal prison some
time before. Finding and capturing him
again had proved to be a long, hard job.
But now Nash was going back to prison.

Because of reports that he had friends who might try to free him, the bureau was taking extra care. Two more special agents and two Kansas City detectives were waiting for the train. Joining Nash's guards, they led the way through the station toward an automobile outside. But they had scarcely left the building when a burst of machine gun fire suddenly filled the air. Taken by surprise in spite of their advance warning, the officers had little chance to defend themselves. For a few moments the machine guns blasted away without mercy. Then they fell silent. Three gunmen jumped into a waiting automobile and sped away. They were hired killers, and their dreadful job was done.

The two detectives and the police chief from Oklahoma were dead. So was a special agent named Raymond Caffrey. Two other agents were badly wounded. Only one man came out unhurt. By a strange twist of fate, that one was not Frank Nash. A stray machine gun bullet had killed him too.

This so-called Kansas City Massacre was a bold and frightening example of the sort of crime that had grown all too common in the United States. The lawless era had begun soon after the end of World War I, when a national prohibition act banned the manufacture or sale of beer, whiskey, and other kinds of liquor. Those who favored the law called Prohibition "the noble experiment," but they soon found that it would not work. Millions of Americans simply refused to give up their beer and whiskey, against the law or not. Almost overnight "bootlegging," the selling of liquor on the sly, grew into a big business controlled by powerful gangs of criminals.

With the huge profits they made, gang leaders were able to bribe local officials. Thus they could do as they pleased with little fear of punishment. Throughout the 1920s—the Roaring Twenties, they were called—this agreement between crooked politicians and the criminal underworld went on, largely unchecked. In many cities, gangsters forced honest storekeepers to pay "protection money" as the price of staying in business. The law had come to mean so little that hoodlums thrived as never before.

Only a few weeks after the Kansas City Massacre, people in the Southwest were shocked by another outrage. This time it was the kidnaping of a wealthy

Oklahoma City oilman by the name of
Charles F. Urschel. Kidnaping was not
yet a federal crime unless the kidnapers
crossed a state line with their victim, but
the Bureau of Investigation made a point
of offering to stand by at once in all
cases. After a week the law assumed
that a state line had been crossed, and
the bureau could then take charge.
(Later laws did away with the waiting
period altogether.) Therefore J. Edgar
Hoover promptly ordered a force of special agents to the Urschel home, though
at first there was little they could do.

A week passed in watchful waiting.
Meanwhile, the kidnapers got in touch
with Urschel's family. A ransom of
$200,000 was paid. The next day Urschel
was released on a lonely country road
near Norman, Oklahoma.

Now at last the special agents could go to work.

Charles Urschel was lucky to be alive, for kidnapers often killed their victims whether or not a ransom was paid. Urschel was a brave man, too. While he was held prisoner, he had kept his wits about him and his ears open, even though he had been blindfolded and handcuffed to a heavy chain. He had overheard conversations, for example, that told him he was in a region suffering from a long dry spell. He knew he had been kept in some kind of farm building, for he had heard chickens cackling and cows lowing. He had noticed that the water given him to drink had an odd taste, and he had had to drink it from a cup with a broken handle. Each morning and evening, too, he had heard airplanes fly overhead. But once, during a rainstorm, there had been no morning plane.

That was not much for the special agents to work with, to be sure. It was enough, though. They began by checking the schedules and flight records on every airline in the area. Then they read the weather reports for the period during which Urschel was held captive. It was a tiresome business, as detective work often is, but it paid off. The agents found that an airliner flying the regular run between Fort Worth and Amarillo, Texas, had indeed been forced off course by a rainstorm one day. And that same rainstorm had ended a long dry spell.

After that it was easy. The trail led to a small ranch near the town of Paradise, Texas. There the agents found a well with water that had an odd taste because

The ranch house near Paradise, Texas, where Charles Urschel was held prisoner.

of minerals in the ground. They found the cup with a broken handle, also, and the chain to which Urschel had been handcuffed.

Faced with that evidence, the ranch owners broke down and confessed. They named others in the kidnap plot with them.

Of the two hoodlums who did the actual kidnaping, one was soon traced to

Colorado, where he gave up without a fight. But the other was George Kelly, a notorious bootlegger and gangster, better known as "Machine Gun" Kelly because he was a dead shot with that weapon. He was thought to be very dangerous, and the special agents were warned to use care in going after him. Nevertheless, they soon found him in Memphis, Tennessee. There, in company with local police officers, they raided his hiding place early one September morning. Caught without his machine gun, Mr. Kelly was not dangerous at all. Trembling with fear, he threw up his hands and begged: "Don't shoot, G-Men, don't shoot!"

They didn't, and Machine Gun Kelly would spend the rest of his days behind prison walls. But he had given the special agents a nickname that stuck. They have been called G-Men—short for Government Men—ever since.

Before the bureau finally closed the Urschel case, 21 people were found guilty of taking part in the kidnap plot. Five of them besides Kelly received life terms in prison. Other sentences varied from several months to ten years. In time, too, special agents got back most of the ransom money.

All in all, it was a job well done.

But it was only one case among many. Crime was on the upswing everywhere, and an angry public demanded action.

Desperate criminal John Dillinger on his way to jail in Indiana. His escape across state lines in March 1934 brought the FBI into the case.

6. G-Men and Public Enemies

Early in March 1934, the newspapers had big, black headlines about John Dillinger. He had just escaped from jail in Crown Point, Indiana, by frightening his jailers with a pistol made of wood. So the stories said, at least. The jailers themselves claimed it was a real gun smuggled in to him by friends.

In either case, the escape made John Dillinger famous and touched off one of the greatest manhunts in the history of the Bureau of Investigation.

Helping himself to two machine guns from the jailhouse, Dillinger stole the sheriff's automobile and drove off to Chicago, where some of his old gang were hiding. He was already a hardened criminal, wanted for bank robbery and murder. Till then, however, Dillinger had broken only state or local laws. But driving his stolen car across the state line from Indiana into Illinois was a federal offense. The G-Men were quickly on his trail.

All of the clues led to Saint Paul, Minnesota. He got away from them there, but they kept after him. With several members of his gang, Dillinger next hid out at a summer resort called the Little Bohemia Lodge, deep in the woods of northern Wisconsin. Surrounding the place in the dead of night, the special agents closed in. Then all at once a dog in the lodge began to bark. The gangsters burst out, machine guns blazing. Amid wild confusion, getaway cars roared down the narrow woodland roads. When at last the shooting stopped, one special agent was dead, another badly wounded. Later it was discovered that a gangster had also died of his wounds.

But John Dillinger had escaped again.

At Washington, J. Edgar Hoover called in Samuel Cowley, one of his top agents. He ordered Cowley to drop everything else, to stay on Dillinger's trail, to get him at all costs.

Dillinger, meanwhile, was back in a Chicago hideout. After a while Cowley succeeded in tracing him there. Melvin Purvis, special agent in charge of the bureau's Chicago office, put every man he could spare on the case. Chicago police joined the hunt for the gangster now known far and wide as Public Enemy Number One. Slowly but surely the net closed around John Dillinger.

In the end he was betrayed by a woman calling herself Anna Sage, with whom he had become friendly. One hot July night she went with him to a movie theater on Chicago's Northwest Side. The G-Men, forewarned, were waiting there. Anna Sage had told them she would wear a red dress so that she and Dillinger could easily be recognized. Sure enough, the agents quickly picked them out among the crowd entering the theater. For fear that innocent people might be hurt if there was any shooting inside, they waited until the show ended, and the couple was leaving. Then the agents moved in. Director Hoover had ordered that Dillinger be taken alive if possible, for that was always the bureau's policy. But John Dillinger refused to be taken. Reaching for the gun in his pocket, he ran toward a nearby alley, then fell to the sidewalk in a hail of bullets. The chase was over.

Curiosity seekers gather about the alley near the Biograph Theater where John Dillinger was killed.

Within a short time Dillinger's whole gang was broken up. It cost some good men's lives, though. Samuel Cowley, for one, was killed trying to arrest a gangster known as "Baby Face" Nelson. But Nelson himself was fatally wounded in the fight. Other gang members either wound up in prison or were shot while resisting arrest.

The tide had begun to turn in the war against gang lawlessness, though the public failed to realize it as yet. A strong movement for a national police force grew in Congress. Some of the leaders there felt that local law enforcement bodies had failed in trying to stop crime. This feeling, indeed, came close to the truth in many cases. The backers of a national police force believed that nothing short of an all-out effort, using the full power of the federal government, could make the country safe again.

J. Edgar Hoover disagreed. In speeches, letters, and personal talks with congressmen, he argued that the local police department was the first line of defense against crime everywhere. Instead of a large and clumsy national police force, he urged better cooperation among all law enforcement bodies: local, state, and federal. As a first step in that direction, he proposed a police training school to be run by the Bureau of Investigation. So it was, in July of 1935, that the National Academy first opened its doors at the U.S. Marine Corps base in Quantico, Virginia.

Twenty-three police officers from different parts of the country made up the first class. Each man had been picked by his own superiors back home. Each paid his own expenses, or had them paid for him by his police department. Tuition at the school was free. The course was made up of twelve weeks of lectures and practical training in all branches of police work.

Other developments followed. Even before Dillinger's death, President Franklin D. Roosevelt had signed several bills passed by the Congress to give the Bureau of Investigation a freer hand in dealing with many kinds of crime. Now, for the first time, special agents were allowed to carry guns and to make arrests. Always before, they had needed special permission to use guns. They had also relied on state or local policemen to make arrests for them.

In that same year of 1935 the bureau

Students at the National Academy at Quantico practice firing from a kneeling position at 200 yards.

received an official new name to go with its new crime-fighting powers. It became the *Federal* Bureau of Investigation— soon to be known simply as the FBI.

The fight went on. One by one, other gangs like Dillinger's were wiped out. Among the worst public enemies of the time were Ma Barker and her four sons. There was very little good in Ma Barker. A born lawbreaker herself, she had trained her boys in crime since childhood. Then, from their home in Missouri's Ozark hill country, the Barkers started on a career of robbery and murder. But they too were losers. G-Men finally trailed them to Florida, and there Ma and one of her sons, Fred, died in a fierce gun battle. Two other sons died as violently as they had lived. The fourth son survived only because he was already in jail for mail robbery.

Another noted hoodlum, Alvin Karpis, had joined Ma Barker in some of her worst crimes. Though he was already a fugitive himself, he sent a bold personal message to J. Edgar Hoover. He was going to kill Hoover, he warned, just as Hoover's men had killed the Barkers. It was a good example of the scorn gangsters felt toward the law in those troubled times. As it happened, the FBI director was already smarting from some recent attacks on him by a well-known U.S. senator. Why, this senator had asked, did J. Edgar Hoover never *personally* arrest any criminal? Now Hoover had his opportunity to answer, and orders went out from FBI headquarters: the director himself would arrest Alvin Karpis.

After some delay word came that Karpis's hideout in New Orleans had been found and was being watched. Hoover flew there at once, with a few selected agents. They found the boastful gangster sitting in his automobile and took him by surprise. Hoover arrested him without so much as a scuffle. A rather comic little problem arose when it was discovered that, somehow, nobody had remembered to bring handcuffs. But a G-Man solved that by whipping off his necktie and tying the gangster's hands with it. Like many others of his kind, Alvin Karpis went to prison for life.

In hundreds of such cases, the forces of the law steadily broke the power of the gangs. Presently the Dillingers, the Machine Gun Kellys, the Ma Barkers,

J. Edgar Hoover, in the foreground, brings Alvin Karpis, Public Enemy Number One, into federal court.

and the rest were no more than bad memories.

As the 1940s opened, however, ugly things were going on in the world outside America. Japan and the United States were close to war over Japanese actions against other nations' rights in the Far East. In Europe war already raged, with Great Britain and Russia fighting for their lives against Nazi Germany. Then on December 7, 1941, Japanese warplanes swooped down on Pearl Harbor, Hawaii, in a sneak attack. Many of our navy's biggest ships were sunk; thousands of American men were killed.

It was the signal for Germany, Japan's ally, to declare war on the United States too. And FBI men had a new kind of trouble on their hands.

7. The Spy Catchers

For a week before the attack on Pearl Harbor, a Japanese submarine prowled silently through Pacific Ocean waters around the Hawaiian island of Oahu. Each day it waited, with only its periscope showing. Each night it rose to the surface, and sharp-eyed lookouts climbed out upon the conning tower. Sometimes the submarine waited in vain. But there were days when the periscope showed white bedsheets hanging on a line by a house near the beach. At night the lookouts often saw lights shining there.

The lights and the bedsheets were signals. Their numbers, and the times of day or night they appeared, stood for code words which in turn were sent by radio to the Japanese navy headquarters in far-off Tokyo. The code words told of the comings and goings of U.S. warships stationed at Pearl Harbor.

It is not certain that the Japanese prepared for their sneak attack in exactly this way. Shortly after the attack, however, a German named Bernard Otto Kuehn confessed that he was the man who made up the code. He said that he had never used it himself. But Kuehn also told how he passed information to the Japanese in many other ways. In fact, special agents of the FBI office in Honolulu had been watching Kuehn for some time past, though they lacked enough evidence to arrest him as long as Germany and the United States were at peace.

Years before the bombs fell on Pearl Harbor, the men of the FBI had worked out a plan of action in case war ever again came to the United States. Old hands in the bureau, from Director Hoover down, were resolved that the mistakes made during World War I should never be made again. And on that tragic December seventh, the plan went into effect at once. Raids by FBI agents working with local police quickly nabbed everyone suspected of spying for Japan, on the U.S. mainland as well as in Hawaii. So swiftly did the raiders strike, in many cases, that secret papers and code books were seized before enemy agents could destroy them. Some gave important details about Japan's whole spy organization, and furnished clues that led to still other enemy agents.

One unfortunate incident marred this achievement. More than a hundred thousand loyal Japanese-Americans living on the Pacific Coast of the United States were also rounded up, torn from homes and businesses, and forced into detention camps in remote areas. They were kept there for the rest of the war. That was done by the army, however, on orders from high government officials. J. Edgar Hoover had opposed the action, and the FBI took no part in it. Afterward, most Americans were ashamed of this injustice, even though they realized it had grown out of panic and blind anger following the sneak attack by Japan.

It was German secret agents, not

Japanese, who proved most troublesome as the war went on.

The German spy masters chose their people carefully and trained them well. Many of those chosen had lived in the United States before the war. They had friends and relatives in this country. They spoke good English. With false identification papers and American money in their pockets, they could easily pass for ordinary citizens and go almost anywhere they pleased. Some were saboteurs, specially trained in the best ways to damage or destroy American factories, as the Germans had done in World War I. Such saboteurs were often put ashore from enemy submarines at night, on lonely stretches of the coast.

German science provided all kinds of devices to fool American counterspies.

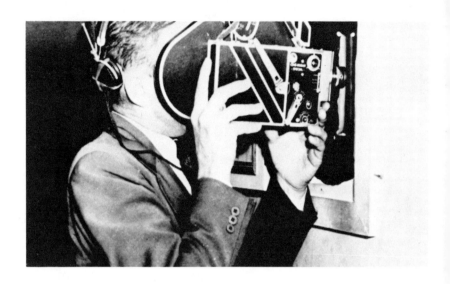

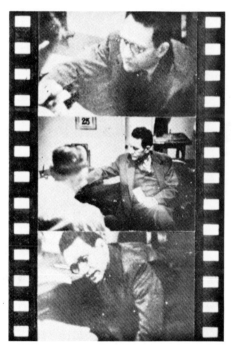

The films shown here are of German spies meeting in a New York apartment during World War II. FBI agents took these films from the apartment next door through a two-way mirror, as seen above. The evidence collected here led to the arrest and conviction of 33 German spies.

A new and secret type of camera, for example, could reduce a whole written or printed page to a tiny dot. Thus a single period at the end of a sentence in some simple little message might contain a spy's orders from Germany, or whatever top-secret information he had to report. Not until the dot was placed under a strong microscope was the true message revealed.

A double agent working for the FBI finally learned the secret. After that the mysterious microdots helped to trap many a spy who had thought he was perfectly safe. Double agents—spies pretending to serve Germany while actually on the side of the United States—were valuable to the bureau on more than one occasion.

Usually, though, catching spies and saboteurs was a matter of endless patience, careful attention to small details, and long, weary hours, days, or even weeks spent in round-the-clock watching of suspects. Countless rumors about spies were reported to the bureau by well-meaning people everywhere. All had to be checked out. Only one rumor in a hundred ever proved to have any truth in it, as FBI men well knew. But that one, traced to its source, might be the means of catching a spy the bureau had never suspected. In the same way, countless little bits and pieces of evidence had to be studied. Each might be worthless by itself. Fitted together with others, however, it might furnish a clue pointing straight to some dangerous saboteur.

A large group of FBI agents spent most of the war in South America, for German spy rings were active in many

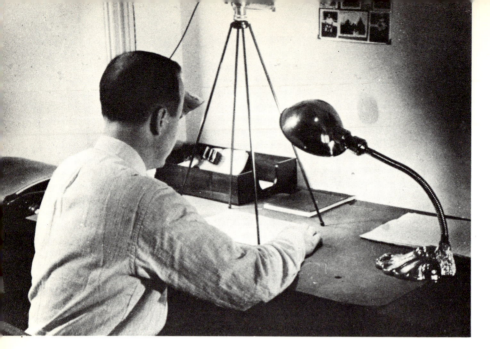

An FBI agent based in Brazil during World War II photographs documents captured in the hunt for spies.

of the countries there. Sometimes the spies kept track of British and American ships, and flashed their movements by radio to lurking German submarines. From South America, too, German spies often tried to slip into the United States by posing as harmless tourists or businessmen. They would undoubtedly have been much more successful than they were, had it not been for the FBI agents who worked with South American governments in blocking their efforts.

FBI special agents were not the only spy catchers, of course. Army, navy, Secret Service men, and others were active too. There was a big job to do, and cooperation got it done. The United States had no Black Tom disasters in World War II. Ninety-one enemy agents were arrested and convicted before the war ended. Some were executed, some sent to prison. A few others fled out of the country before they could be caught. But not one was able to carry out an important mission.

Germany surrendered in May 1945. Japan fought on till August. Then a powerful new weapon, the atomic bomb, forced her to surrender too. Peace had come to the world again—or had it?

8. Another Kind of War

Hard-pressed by Nazi Germany in World War II, Russia had welcomed the United States as an ally. But Russia's Communist rulers had never changed their long-range plans. Secretly they were still the sworn enemies of all democratic nations, just as young J. Edgar Hoover had reported more than 25 years before. So it was not long after the end of the war that world peace was disturbed by a new outbreak, this time between the U.S. and Russia. It was not a shooting war. Officially, both countries remained friendly. The Cold War, so called, was fought with bluffs and threats of force, and by spies and traitors working behind the scenes. But this, too, was a contest no free country could afford to lose.

Among the FBI's new Cold War duties was the investigation of all government employees suspected of belonging to the Communist Party. That soon led to trouble, for most Americans disliked the idea of their government poking and prying into people's private lives.

Once again, as in the long-ago days of Theodore Roosevelt, the bureau was called a secret police force. The men in power in the government were accused of using it to ruin the reputations of their political enemies. Some people felt real concern that the FBI had become too powerful for the nation's good. Arguments grew bitter on both sides. Many a plain citizen, confused by everything he read or heard, believed that the bureau was deciding who could and who could not have government jobs.

Actually, the FBI had no power to hand down such decisions. No FBI man ever had sought that power. Investigations were made only when ordered by the attorney general or the president of the United States, or requested by the head of some government department. Then the bureau's job was the collecting of evidence, nothing more.

Quietly, through all the sound and fury, the FBI went on doing that job. Then, little by little, the truth about Communism in America began to be recognized.

A man named Whittaker Chambers confessed that he had once been a Communist, and a spy for Russia. But, said he, when he came to understand what Communism really stood for, he changed his mind. He told all this to a congressional committee. Chambers also declared that Alger Hiss, a brilliant young official in the U.S. Department of State, had helped him steal secret government papers and turn them over to the Russians. Hiss denied the charges. His superiors in the Department of State backed him up. They told of his fine record. To a man, they said that they trusted and respected him.

Plainly, either Hiss or Chambers was lying. It was up to special agents of the FBI to find out which.

Link by link, they uncovered a chain

of evidence pointing to Alger Hiss. Whittaker Chambers produced some of the stolen documents. Among them were papers in Hiss's handwriting. Others had been copied on a typewriter he owned. The agents found evidence that Hiss had loaned money to Chambers, though he denied it. Hiss also denied that he had ever been in Chambers's home. After a

In a dramatic moment at the committee hearings, Alger Hiss (right) and Whittaker Chambers (left) meet face to face.

long search, the agents found a maid who had seen both him and his wife there. And so it went.

In a federal courtroom, late in 1949, Alger Hiss was convicted of perjury, the legal term for lying under oath.

At about the same time a jury in New York City found eleven top leaders of the American Communist Party guilty of "teaching ... the overthrow of the United States Government by force and violence." The battle in that courtroom had been months long, and bitterly fought. Nor did it end there. Appeals by the Communists' lawyers finally took the case to the U.S. Supreme Court. There too the verdict of guilty was upheld.

Here again, the bulk of the evidence that stood up so well had been gathered by special agents of the FBI.

Even before Alger Hiss went to trial, bureau men were busy on another dangerous gap in the nation's security. Somehow, Russian agents had stolen the secret of the atomic bomb, most terrible weapon ever known. An investigation led to one Klaus Fuchs, a British scientist who had worked with Americans on the original atomic project. British intelligence agents, warned by the FBI, arrested Fuchs. He confessed. Still, though, the case could not be closed. An American had been involved in the spy plot too, but Klaus Fuchs knew hardly anything about him. The description he gave might have fitted almost anyone. He did remember, however, that the man had seemed to know a little about chemistry.

Slim though the lead was, it was a start. A sister of Fuchs, who lived in

Massachusetts, was questioned. She had taken no part in her brother's spying, but it turned out she too had seen the man of mystery. He had called at her home and asked for Klaus Fuchs. She had forgotten his name, but she remembered that he had once mentioned something about chemistry. Then a special agent found the name, Harry Gold, in the records of an earlier investigation of Communist activities. There had been little evidence against Gold, whoever he was—but the records described him as a chemist.

The agents found Harry Gold in Philadelphia. At first he denied everything. Then he broke down and confessed. Unlike Klaus Fuchs, he was able to tell about several fellow plotters. One was a former sergeant in the U.S. Army named David Greenglass, who had worked on the atomic project at Los Alamos, New Mexico. When arrested, Greenglass also talked freely. The other members of the ring, he said, were his sister Ethel and her husband, Julius Rosenberg. That closed the case at last.

One of the most tragic things about the affair was that all these people had truly believed they were helping to make the world a better place by turning traitor for Russia. Many of them finally realized their mistake, but much too late. Both Rosenbergs were tried, convicted, and put to death for treason. The rest all served long prison terms.

The Cold War went on.

In 1957, FBI men smashed still another Russian spy ring by arresting Colonel Rudolf Abel in New York City. Abel, a

These innocent-looking objects were hollow. Abel
used them to smuggle out microfilmed messages.

professional spy with years of experience
in many different countries, was by far
the most skillful enemy agent to be
caught in the United States. He was sent
to prison, but exchanged less than five
years later for the pilot of a U.S. spy
plane that had been shot down over
Russia.

The Russians too had their Cold War
victories!

9. The Watch Goes On

"The reward of good work is more good work to do." So an old saying goes, and so it is for the FBI. The years following the letup in the Cold War brought new criminals, new kinds of crime—and new problems for the bureau.

FBI men helped in the long fight of black Americans to win their civil rights under the laws of the United States. They still do, as that fight goes on. FBI men were called upon to help stop the hijackers: modern-day pirates who threatened the lives of thousands of airline passengers. Every day, FBI men are engaged in a silent war against criminal groups that are often richer, more powerful—and smarter, too—than the old-time gangs of the Roaring Twenties. And so it goes. The job of law enforcement never ends.

On Pennsylvania Avenue in Washington, D.C., is the busy headquarters of the FBI. This is the nerve center of a modern crime-fighting organization that reaches out into every corner of the nation.

Here the director and other top executives have their offices. Here are the famous FBI Laboratory and the fingerprint files by which some 200,000,000 people—both known criminals and law-abiding citizens—can be identified within

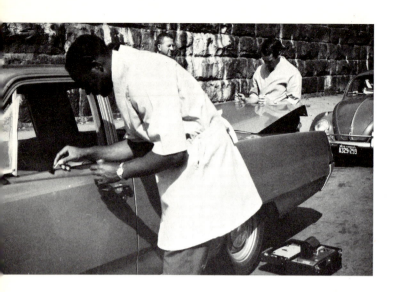

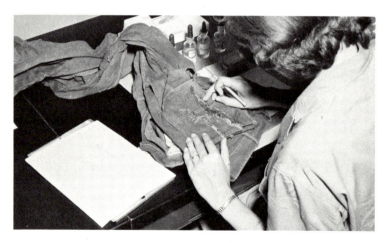

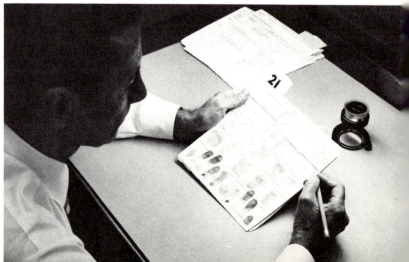

minutes, anywhere in the United States. Here also are the secret files holding information collected over many years in FBI investigations bearing on national security. And here is the place where a new recruit begins his career as a special agent of the bureau.

Agents come from every state of the Union, and from many different walks of life. The old rule that no one but a lawyer or an accountant could be accepted

At FBI headquarters in Washington, D.C. (from top left to bottom right) technicians process a car for fingerprints; match a piece of cloth to a torn pair of trousers; check fingerprints; and compare a plaster cast of a tire print with the tire of a suspect's car.

was dropped long ago, for it takes a wide range of knowledge and skills to fulfill the bureau's responsibilities in the modern world. There are over 7,000 special agents in today's FBI. They include men and women trained in science, engineering, and foreign languages, among others.

No matter what his background, however, every recruit must complete eighteen weeks of difficult training before he goes out into the field. Part of the course takes place in classrooms, with long-time veterans of the bureau serving as teachers. Here the recruit learns the basic skills of detective and investigation work. Then he is sent to the FBI Academy at the U.S. Marine Corps base in Quantico, Virginia. The training there is rugged. It consists of thorough instruction in all kinds of firearms, plus coaching in the various forms of hand-to-hand fighting. An FBI agent may be called on to face death in the line of duty at any time. It is the bureau's policy to see that he is as well fitted to protect himself as possible.

Quantico is still the scene, too, of the National Academy established in 1935 to train local police officers. Nearly a hundred specially selected men attend two twelve-week courses each year. Though many large cities now have police training programs of their own, the National Academy is still famed as one of the best in the world.

But to return to our FBI recruit: Once through his training, the new agent is given his badge and identification card and assigned to his first field office. He will be on probation until that office's special agent in charge—SAC for short —is satisfied with his work. Throughout his service with the bureau, supervisors will keep a close check on his conduct, and call him to account for any slip-ups. The rules are stern, but experience has proved their value. Over the years, very few special agents have ever been found guilty of dishonesty or neglect of duty. That record is carefully guarded.

"One man didn't build the FBI," J. Edgar Hoover often said, "but one man can tear it down."

The FBI has 59 field offices, located in large cities in every state. Besides these, smaller offices in outlying areas surround each field office. Thus the FBI is always within reach of almost any community in the United States. All offices keep in

FBI agents in training: firing from the 25-yard line on the ranges at Quantico (right); learning defensive tactics at FBI headquarters (below).

touch with one another and with FBI headquarters, not only by telephone and teletype but by a special radio network as well. FBI automobiles are also tied into the network. In an emergency, therefore, information and orders can be flashed instantly to any office, and special agents sent wherever they are needed without loss of time.

This ability to cover trouble spots quickly is an FBI strong point. The bureau's efficient organization is another. Every type of crime—kidnaping, espionage, bank robbery, and so on right down the line—is handled by a separate division at headquarters. When a crime is reported from the field, the report goes at once to the proper division. There it is carefully examined by experts. Details of the crime are compared with those of other, similar crimes described in the FBI records. Perhaps a pattern will show up, to narrow the list of possible suspects. If so, it will often put the special agents handling the case on the trail of some known criminal, saving time and effort that might otherwise be wasted in following false leads.

Together, the records of these crime divisions are known as the FBI National Crime Information Center. In recent years the material has all been placed on the memory banks of computers for the fastest possible reference. Like the FBI Laboratory and the fingerprint files, it is always open to state and local police departments.

J. Edgar Hoover died in 1972. He had served as director of the FBI for 48 years: a long time indeed for one man

J. Edgar Hoover's strong leadership for more than forty years made the FBI one of the best-known crime-fighting organizations in the world and set the pattern for the years to come.

to head a government bureau. Throughout those years of steady growth, he had made the FBI an organization wholly devoted to loyalty and respect for the law —as he himself was. And over that long span both Hoover and the bureau sometimes aroused bitter criticism. Yet the chief concern of the harshest critics did not come to pass; the FBI never became a secret police force threatening the rights of the people. That held true during more than half a century of service to the nation, often in times of great trouble and change.

It will go on holding true for as long as free Americans believe in justice and obedience to the law.

Index

Nash, Frank, 38, 39, 40
National Academy, Quantico, Virginia, 55–56, 87
National Crime Information Center, 91
Nelson, Lester Gillis (Baby Face), 54

Palmer, A. Mitchell, 20 (pic), 21–22
Palmer's raids, 21–22
Pearl Harbor, 61, 62–63, 64
Prohibition, 40, 41
Purvis, Melvin, 51

Quantico, Virginia, 55, 86–87

Roosevelt, Franklin D., 56
Roosevelt, Theodore, 4 (pic), 5, 6, 8, 9, 26, 73
Rosenberg, Ethel, 80
Rosenberg, Julius, 80

Sabotage
  World War I, 11, 12 (pic), 13, 14–15, 16
  World War II, 65–66, 69, 70, 71
Sage, Anna, 52
Secret Service, 7, 8, 14, 71

Spies
  Abel, Rudolf, 80–81
  Fuchs, Klaus, 78, 79
  Gold, Harry, 79
  Greenglass, David, 80
  Kuehn, Bernard Otto, 63
  Rosenberg, Ethel, 80
  Rosenberg, Julius, 80
Spying, 14, 16, 65–66, 67 (pic), 68, 69, 81 (pic)
State, Department of, 75
Stone, Harlan Fiske, 28, 29, 33, 36, 37
Supreme Court, 77

Taft, William Howard, 10
Treasury Department, 7

Urschel, Charles F., 42, 43–45, 47

World War I
  draft evaders, 16
  enemy aliens, 15
  military deserters, 15–16
  sabotage during, 11, 12, 14–15
World War II
  Japanese-American raids, 65
  spying during, 62–63, 68, 70